D1321956

Spoonface Steinberg

Lee Hall's extraordinary, award-winning play about faith, love and the meaning of life was first broadcast on Radio 4 in 1997 to unprecedented acclaim. A monologue by an autistic eight-year-old girl who is dying of cancer, it touched the hearts of all who heard it. This stage version opened at the Crucible Theatre, Sheffield, before transferring to the New Ambassadors Theatre, London, in January 2000.

'It would be a stone heart that could not squeeze a tear, if not for Spoonface, then for ourselves . . .' Lyn Gardner, *Guardian*

Lee Hall's theatre work includes translations of Buchner's *Leonce and Lena* (Gate Theatre), Brecht's *Mr Puntila and his Man Matti* (The Right Size/Almeida, Traverse and West End), *Mother Courage and her Children* (Shared Experience), and *A Servant to Two Masters* (RSC & Young Vic). His adaptation of his award-winning radio play *Spoonface Steinberg* opened at the New Ambassadors Theatre in January 2000 and a new stage play *Cooking With Elvis* – originally the radio play *Blood Sugar* – opens in the West End. Lee is currently filming *Dancer*, directed by Stephen Daldry, and will shortly be filming an adaptation of his prize-winning radio play *I Love You Jimmy Spud*. His television work includes *The Student Prince* and *Spoonface Steinberg*.

Lee Hall

Spoonface Steinberg

Methuen Drama

Published by Methuen Drama

3 5 7 9 1 0 8 6 4

First published in Great Britain in 1997 by BBC Books

This edition published in 2000 by
Methuen Publishing Ltd

A CIP catalogue record is available from the British Library

ISBN 0 413 74870 7

Typeset by MATS, Southend on Sea, Essex
Printed and bound in Great Britain by
Cox & Wyman Ltd, Reading, Berkshire

Caution

All rights whatsoever in this play are strictly reserved and application for
performance etc. should be made to:
The Rod Hall Agency Ltd, 7 Goodge Place, London W1P 1FL.
No performance may be given unless a licence has been obtained.

Spoonface Steinberg

Spoonface Steinberg was broadcast on Radio 4 in January 1997. It was directed by Kate Rowland and performed by Becky Simpson. This stage version premiered at the Crucible Theatre, Sheffield, in December 1999 and transferred to the New Ambassadors Theatre, London, in January 2000. The cast was as follows:

Spoonface Steinberg   Kathryn Hunter

Director Marcello Magni
Co-director Anne Castledine
Designer Liz Cooke
Lighting designer Tina McHugh

The music in the play is taken from *Callas: La Divina* 1 and 2 (EMI Classics).

MUSIC: *Maria Callas singing 'Casta Diva' from* Norma *by Bellini*

(Spoonface talks over the music)

Spoonface: In the olden days – when they wrote the songs and the operas and that, it mattered how you died – when the singers singed and went about – and they sang like beautiful birds and they fell over and everything – and she was all quavery and beautiful and everyone holded their breath – and there she was in the special light with her boobs and everything – and everyone would be looking and they would cry and in their hearts they would weep for the poor lady – the poor poor lady who dies so well.

And if I could ever grow up I would be one of them sad singers and do the dying and everybody would clap and cheer – and in all of the singing when people heard it they would have a little piece of beauty – which is very important – to have the little piece of beauty what's in the music – and this is what I realised – even though the beautiful singing is sad – it is still happy in a way – the saddest things fill you up – like in a big way and you feel so full as in no happiness can bring such – and all such sadness is beautiful – as beautiful as the singing – as beautiful as the dying – and it would make a meaning – and I would sing the dying and people would love me – and I would sing the dying and out come the angels to take me away – and I would sing the dying and there would be a lovely piece of beauty in the world – and I would sing the dying and be as free as a little bird floating up to heaven.

MUSIC: *Maria Callas singing 'Casta Diva' from* Norma

I never heard such singing before except for when Doctor Bernstein brought the tapes – even though the other children like such music as Take That and that – even one little girl has this tape of Take That and Take That sent her this picture and they were all blowing her a kiss and all she ever does is play the music and she can't even hear because she is in a coma and then Take That made her a tape which said 'Hello this is Robbie' and she still wasn't better – and I said this was no surprise on account of the tape – but I play the

proper music – it is so sad – and it is about the
dying and it makes me so clear.

   I was never right ever since I was born – this
means that I do very bad writing and that I can't
speak proper and that I am backwards and that I
am a special child – but why is a mystery for
what they have not got an answer – but Mam said
when I was born it was at a dark night and it was
raining and thundery and all the cats and dogs
and things were under the tables – and the wind
was screeching round everywhere – and everything was quite horrible – but I didn't mind
because I was just little and I was in the hospital
and Mam kissed me and when she looked at my
face she noticed that it was round – and everyone
came and looked at my face – and they laughed
and said I was Spoonface because when they
looked at my face it was round as a spoon and
when you look into a spoon you see this face just
like mine – and that is how I came to be
Spoonface Steinberg – because my other name is
Steinberg – but I never even knew because I was
just a little baby and all the stars and planets were
moving inside of me and I was looking up and
the world was as bright as colours and as shim-
mery as light and I was just a baby – and when

you're a baby you have a soft head and that – and that's what makes you backwards. Sometimes when it's very late at night – when they think I'm asleep, Mam says to Dad that maybe it is his fault that I am not right – on the fact that on the day Dad came back when he was out with the floozie, I did fall off the chair – Dad came back and it was quite late for our tea and I was sitting on the chair and Mam said that Dad was out with someone – and Dad says he was in the office doing the meeting – and Mam said she phoned the meeting and he was off with the office doing a floozie – and that this was one of his students – and she was going somewhere – off with the final straw – then there was all this crying and scream-ing and Dad went like a beetroot and Mam said that the student was just a baby and had big boobs and I fell over – it was like when you bump your head only worse – and then every-thing went white like lightening – and this was bad on account of my softness – and they were crying there with me and I was silent as a worm – and Dad told Mam he would not ever have another floozie if Mam would be nicer and Mam said she would be nicer – and then it was that everything was alright – except I started going backwards – but I am not sure if this is to do with

it or not – maybe it is – maybe it is not – I think
I was backwards before the fall – before Dad
came back and everything – I think I was always
backwards ever since I was born and there was all
the thunder and that, and I think ever since I was
born that my brain was quite special – I think I
have a special brain what is quite different in how
it was and stuff – but nobody knows for sure – all
the experts with all their computers and all the
doctors who poke in your ear and look into your
brain and all the people who do the quizzes and
all questioners and such like – none of them
know for certain – they all said no one can know
can ever know for certain – and that's what Dad
says – he says there is only one thing for certain –
nobody knows anything for certain – what is true
I think – on account that he is a lecturer of
philosophy – the thing is even now I am old I
cannot read proper or to write and am very bad
at games and that I cannot go to a proper school
as I am not allowed on account of my brain – but
I am quite a special little girl, though – that's what
Mrs Spud says – Mrs Spud does the cleaning –
and she says that I am quite one of the special
girls she has ever known and every time she
comes she brings me a sweetie which is very nice
for she has so many problems of her own – she

says that everybody is different and that it is quite good indeed and that we should all be happy and that – for every person is a very special person and that it is good to be different as if there's no difference we would all be the same – and Mrs Spud told me not to worry about my brain because to be different is to be who you are – so I do not believe that I fell on my head – I do not believe that I was affected – or it was Dad's fault for the floozie or Mam's fault 'cos I was unattended – I believe that I was supposed to be backward – I believe it was all part of what is supposed to be – and when I was born God came and touched me on my head – down he came and touched my soft spot and made me me.

MUSIC: *Maria Callas singing 'Mon cœur s'ouvre à ta voix' from* Samson et Dalila *by Saint-Saëns*

One day I started to do the numbers. This was when Dad came back from the university and he was with a calculator for doing the marks. He was sat doing the marks when he said two numbers and I went 42 – because it was the answer of the two numbers – and then he goes – goodness me – and then he said two more numbers and I said 147 – which was another answer – and then he did more and more – and some of the answers he had to do on the calculator – and then he started shouting of Mam – and Mam came running as if there was something bad – but it was only me doing the numbers and I did more and more – and Mam kissed me and was crying and that – and Dad kept doing more and more and he was laughing – and Mam said he had to stop – and I said what was it that had made her cry? – and she said that it was because of the numbers and never in the world did they know I could do the numbers – but I could do them now – and I was a genius – and it was of my brain.

And then I had to do them in front of a doctor – and then the doctor said – if Spoonface can do numbers then she can do dates – and then I did some – this is how I do it – what is the day of July the 4th 2010? – Saturday – amazing, absolutely amazing – and that is how I do the dates and they have to look it up in a book as soon as I've said the answer and there it is – and they say how do I know so many numbers? and I say I don't know – and how do I know so many dates? – and I also say I don't know – but it's just obvious like colours – and that is why – and Mrs Spud says that is why we are all different – to me the numbers are obvious and to her some other stuff is obvious – like how to clean the loo and that – but at least that means we're all different.

So this is all because I am autistic – and that is quite a big strain on Mam and Dad which was account of why they did split up – for a start Mam was quite sad – she was in the house when Dad went to work and she did look at her books and such like as she was getting a Ph.D. also like Dad – only he finished quicker on account of women have to have babies that men can't have – this meant that her's was much slower – and she would sit in the room and when ever she was just to do some work I came in and then she had to stop – and it wasn't fair of me to do the Ph.D. – and Dad was on the committees – so Mam had to drink the vodka – and she used to sit with the book and the vodka – and Dad came back and she said – that he was not of attention – and maybe he wasn't.

Then one day Dad said he had met one person who was doing a different Ph.D. to Mam and that she was very nice and that he would go away to live with her for a bit – and Mam said she was glad of him to go – and even though I was backwards and that – it would be better than his stupid face – and off Dad went for a bit until sometimes he came back for a few minutes on a Saturday.

Then Mam used to have more and more – and she would come to me and say 'My poor sweet angel, my poor sweet angel' – and then drink the vodka – and then she had to take tablets off the Doctor and would stop the vodka at the same time – except one time she had the pills and the vodka and went to sleep on the stair and I put on her a nice blanket in case anyone tripped – but nobody did trip as there was only me – then the next day Mrs Spud came and tidied up where she had been sick.

MUSIC: *Maria Callas singing 'Teneste la promessa' from* La Traviata *by Verdi*

When I first started feeling funny that is when I still had hair – it was hardly noticeable at first – that was there was hardly nothing wrong except I was tired a bit – but then Mam was very worried that I was thinner and thinner and one day I might fade away to a speck – and that I was looking peaky – but because I'm backwards then

I wasn't very good at saying what is wrong – so
she took me straight to the doctor in case I disap-
peared – and the doctor looked at me like this
. . . and he said – 'Oh deary me, Spoonface will
have to go straight to the hospital' – which is
where I went – it was alright as I had been before
to do the numbers – they were all very nice to
me and the doctors held on to my hand and stuff
and they all smiled which means something is
wrong – and then Mam looked greyish and they
said they were going to have to put me in a tube,
which was quite horrible as I am only little – I
did not wish to go into the tube but they said I
would have to on account of being so thin – and
inside the tube they would find out what it was –
so I went in the tube and Mam was watching
when I went in and waved bye bye – and then all
these computers went off and stuff – and they did
all this dialling and whirring and then there was
some rays or something – and I was in there like
it was a space machine but it never went any-
where except in the hospital even though it took
ages – and I waited and all the computers were
doing different numbers and all the information
was going everywhere and that – and then it
came time for me to come out and when I came
out there was Mam and the doctor waiting and

they said hello and I was allowed out – the doctor said he would have to check the switches and that we should all go into a room where Mam could cry and I could play with Lego – when I was in the room I got a drink of pop and Mam said it was unexpected that we would go straight to the hospital and go into a tube – then the doctor came back and said that he had got an answer off the machines and the answer was – that I was going to die.

MUSIC: *Maria Callas singing 'Addio, del passato' from* La Traviata *by Verdi*

Mam looked very sad and said the doctors must have wonky computers and that they needed to put me in the tube again – but then they said how the computers were only new and that they were very expensive and that it was definite what they said – and it was that I was still going to die – only they said there was hope – that there was always hope – and anyway, it would take a long time for me to die so we went home for some tea – when we went home in the car there was rain and wind and everything and we passed this accident where a man on a motorbike had got his head smashed off – and Mam said that even if I

was supposed to die there would still be hope
'cos there was millions of people that were saved
by God everyday – even if the poor man was
smashed on the road – and so it was better not be
too worried about it – so I said I wasn't worried
and we had fish fingers.

Then Mam had to phone Dad – he was with
the granduate – in a little flat and everything –
and Mam rang and the granduate answered and
said that she would still like to meet Mam as
there was no hard feelings but Mam said she had
to speak to Dad quick – normally she used to
shout at him saying, 'What did I do? What did I
do?' – but this time she said to the granduate to
get right off as she needed to talk to Dad imme-
diately – then on came Dad and Mam said there
was something terrible wrong with Spoonface
and that she'd been in a tube and had been play-
ing with the Lego and they said she was going to
die and he must come at once – and then she put
the phone down – and Dad came and said this
was the last thing he expected – especially as we
had so many troubles and he kissed me and he
also kissed Mam and said – what such troubles
we had – first I wasn't born right, and that even
though I did numbers, I wasn't very good at

games and stuff – and then he went off with a graduand too young for him and stuff and Mam was living here with only me – and now I was going to die.

Mam said she was sorry and that deep down she really loved Dad, and Dad was sorry that he really loved Mam and they all loved me over and over – I was supposed to be asleep by now but I could hear them and of everything they said – it was so terrible for everyone and this was the change of everything – and then they came in at the door and looked at me in the dark where I was supposed to be asleep – and I was lying in my beautiful bed with all the covers up and they would stare like this at me . . . and have their arms holding each other and they whispered that I was a poor little soul – but they never knew I was wide awake and I could see them through the crack in my eye as not to scare them – and when I looked at them and I saw that they were crying – and then Dad said: there I was fast asleep not a care in the world – but this was ridiculous because I was there awake all the time.

MUSIC: *Maria Callas singing 'Ebben? ne andrò lontana' from* La Wally *by Catalani*

After a while Dad came back to see us quite a bit – some nights he used to stay in Mam's bed and everything and he would see me in the morning – and the Ph.D. said that she had a new boyfriend who was quite young and played in a musical group and that Dad was quite old to be living at her house and Dad was to live all alone except when he came to see us – and when he came he was nicer than ever – and Mam was quite happy sometimes but she would cry at night when I couldn't hear who she was – I kept going to the hospital and they would do all these checks on me and go, 'Oh well, it is very bad indeed' – Mam would be worried and tell me to be brave – then one day they said, 'Spoonface is going to die, except we might put her in this machine and she would get some rays and stuff and then she would be better' – but I couldn't go in straight away on account of the list so I waited a few days and stuff – and Dad came round every night and that – and he said that Mam was to go out to see her friend and he would stay and watch me – but he never 'cos he was downstairs and he found Mam's vodka – I was feeling quite sickly and I was all wobbly because I was thin as a stick so I went straight to bed – then I was asleep – then there was this

noise and in came Dad and he smelt really weird
– and he came right up to my nose – like he has
flying over my nose which was horrible – and
his eyes were sort of fat and soft – and he had
one of the glasses from downstairs and the vodka
what Mam kept in the freezer – and he took this
huge gulp and went pink – I just looked at him
like this – wishing Mam was back – then he
grabbed my arm and it was quite hard – he did
grab me tight like this . . . and I looked up and
was frightened of what he would do – and then
I thought I was going to faint of the pressure –
and he started rocking backwards like this – and
then he said I had suffered the worse out of anyone in the world and it was all his fault – that he
didn't know what he was doing – that he was
such a young man and he was just a poor philosophy man because he couldn't think of what else
to do – and that he loved Mam even though
when they had such a young baby as myself it
was before things were settled – but then he said
that he loved me and he didn't know what he
was doing except for that he was sorry for it all –
and especially sorry for his whole life – but then
I was Spoonface from his own sperm and that I
was the most loved child in the whole world –
and even if I never understood a word I was still

the most loved child in all the world – and he
went like this for ages – and all of a sudden he
stopped doing his grip and fell backwards and
plopped on to the floor – I wanted to go to the
loo, but I didn't ask in case he tried to grab me
again – and I saw he was sitting back like this
. . . on the floor and his face was bright red and
he sort of shook – he was shaking and he did
these gasps like he couldn't breathe – and no
tears would come from his crying just these
shakes – then I heard the door and Mam came
up the stairs in her coat and she saw Dad on the
floor doing the shaking and she just left him and
picked me out of bed and put me in between
her bosoms and she pressed me there for a long
time and kissed the tip of my head – after that
she took me to her room – she said that Dad was
over-whelmed and that he was reading of
Kierkegaard which was too bad for him – and
the next day I was in Mam's bed and Dad was in
mine.

And she said that not to worry about Dad that
he was very sorry from gripping me so hard and
it was all 'cos of the vodka – and he promised he
would never shake again.

MUSIC: *Maria Callas singing 'O mio babbino caro'*
from Gianni Schicchi *by Puccini*

I love the beautiful women who do the operas
and how they sing and they flutter their voices
like this – because it is the saddest things are the
best things of all – and that is because God made
all the sad things for to make us human and this
is what Doctor Bernstein said at the hospital
when I went in – he was quite old and stuff and
he said that I was very brave and I should be very
brave because when his Mam was little she was
very brave as well even though she was in a concentration camp.

Concentration camps were these places where
they took Jewish people to burn – this is what
the doctor said – he said that there were loads of
people and they all had to sleep on one bunk and
that – and the Nazis shot them and then they
starved them and it was horrible for his poor
Mam because she was just little – in the whole
history of the world there has never been anything as awful as the concentration camps, but
what happened to the poor people there was to
show that they never gave up hope – and that
never mind the worse thing that could happen to

people they could not stop them from being human beings – some of the little children were skinnier than I am now with the cancer, and all that was wrong with them was they didn't eat – just this soup what didn't have any vegetables in it – and they'd just be standing there and their Mammies and Daddies would be bashed – like there was one little girl who was with her Mam and the soldier came and hit her Mam on the head and shot her and then she died and the poor little girl just had to stand there – that little girl was the Mam of the doctor – and there were millions and millions of people like this – so in comparison to me it is much worse – and I felt sorry for the doctor when he told me these things as he had a little cry in the corner of his eye – and he never said any of this to scare me – he said all of this to help me because the whole lesson of the stories was that little children were braver than everybody else *(underneath her voice we hear Maria Callas singing 'Casta Diva' and then 'Mon cœur s'ouvre à ta voix')* and all the little children all played games in the middle of mud – in the middle of the concentration camp they played – and this was the human spirit – in the middle where their Mams and Dads was getting gassed – and they could kill their Mams and stuff but they couldn't kill what was in the minds of the children – this was the lesson – that no matter how bad it is for us while we are dying it is still a wonderful thing that we are alive – this is what the doctor said – and he said when the soldiers came and took the poor little children to the ovens and the poor children and everything thought they were going for a wash but everybody knew really that they were going to get gassed – because they had seen the smoke of burning bodies – then the children were waiting outside and all the little children wrote things on the walls – on the walls of the gas chamber where they were about to be cooked. And some little children wrote poems – and some little children drew pictures – and even today you can see the pictures of butterflies on the outside – little butterflies that were flying up to God – beautiful butterflies with tender wings that would brush their faces and kiss them better before they flew – careful little butterflies in all the death and the mud and every thing – and that day when he told me this I cried for the butterflies and the little children – and all their sad faces drifting up to heaven.

And the doctor said that his Grandma used to be a singer of the opera before she went to this place – and in them days everyone loved the opera – not like now when everyone likes Take That – and when they would put the lights out – all the poor women on the bunks would think of their husbands who were never to be seen – and they would ask Grandma Bernstein to sing – and in the sad dark she would sing – sing to all the poor skinny women – and she sang all the songs what she knew in the opera – and she sang for the poor people in the bunks – and all the poor people who had died – and she sang for the children of the people to come – and that was very important to everyone to have such songs to be sung – and then I would play the music and in the heart of it I could hear the singing of the poor Grandma on her bunk – and the poor children who wrote their pictures on the wall – and even in the darkest place there was someone with such a beautiful song to sing.

MUSIC: *Maria Callas singing 'O mio babbino caro' from* Gianni Schicchi

By the time I had to go into the machine I was quite upset that I was going to die but then

Mam told me not to be because it would zap me
and then I would be alright – but I knew that
maybe there was a chance that I would not be
zapped proper – but I never said anything – so I
went in and got zapped – I went in every day for
three weeks they said that was quite enough as
they didn't want to zap too much as they might
do a mischief – they gave me centigrays – these
are special rays which get the cancer and make it
better – they put me in the machine and then
zapped the centigrays straight into me – and I
felt so small as if I was travelling all through the
history of time to another place where all the
things were different – and in this place then
everybody was laughing and happy and there was
no more hospitals or concentration camps and
everybody had ice cream and watched the telly
and there was opera people and everything – and
all of a sudden I believed that maybe I had died
in the zapper and when I looked around that I
was in heaven – but then I came out and I had
not died at all and I was still in the hospital and
there was Mam and Doctor Bernstein and I
remembered this was the hospital and there were
concentration camps and I was still going to die
– and then everybody said how I was – and I
said quite well – and they said what a brave little

girl I was in the zapper and that I should have a
special little present – and that it was a special
CD player what the nurses had bought me 'cos
they knew I liked the opera – but I couldn't
wear it inside the machine on account of the
interference – after a few days they told me the
zapper was not really such a zapper at all – and
in fact it was called an accelerator – which
means to go very fast – but it is for to slow the
cancer down – and I sat for hours – but the cancer never slowed – in fact that the centigrays
hardly stopped it at all – and they said I had to
go home for a while.

  I started getting even worse than I was – really
woozy and everything and virtually as soon as I
had got out of the hospital they said I had to go
back in – this time they said there'd be no more
machines and stuff – but they would give me this
special thing in my arm and that would make me
sick and have diarrhoea and all my hair would
fall out – this was the chemicals and such and
they said that if that didn't save me, that was that
– so I went and had the diarrhoea – and they
put the thing in my arm – like a tap which they
had all bags and special machines which had
these chemicals that they put in my arm and

made me ill – I was feeling quite sickly and then
I had to have this medicine to stop me puking
up – it is quite hard to have the diarrhoea and
want to puke up at the same time because you
don't know which one to do first – and this was
called a side-effect – but it effected all over – and
I would sit in the bed with the arm thing and
my new CD and then I would poo myself and
my hair all fell out and I was quite weird – then
one day Dad came and he had this hat for me to
wear it had a picture of these opera singers on
the front and I wore the hat even though I was
inside – and everyday I was sicker and sicker and
I goes to God – Please God, why are you making me so sickly? – and I never found out –
because he never said – then I was quite
depressed – and my eyebrows fell out.

Doctor Bernstein came to see how I was and he
said it must be horrible having diarrhoea – but I
said I didn't mind that much, and anyway that's
what Beethoven had when he wrote his music – he
had diarrhoea and deafness – and he was quite ill a
lot of the time – but he wrote the beautiful music
– and the doctor said how did I know such things
and I said someone told me what looked at my
tapes.

Then Doctor Bernstein said there was this man, Job, and he had a horrible time except he put up with it and he was alright. Doctor Bernstein said that Job was a Jew too and so was Jesus and so was all these famous people – and that there was a lot to suffer in the history of the world – which is true – and one day he came to me and took off the drip and said that the good news was that my hair would grow – but the bad news was I was still full of cancer and there was nothing to be done – all the chemicals and the centigrays and everything was useless.

When I went home I was in bed a lot and I used to watch everything through the window – and had lots of time to be by myself and think about things and that.

First – when Mam brought me home, then Mam said that I was a brave little girl indeed because of my baldness and everything and that my hair would be growing in soon – but then when there was Dad there and that he was allowed to stay on the sofa downstairs for every day that I was alive – then I was in bed and then I would have the pills and stuff which is called morphine – and I would be propped so I would

look out of the window – then she said that she
did hate God and how could he do such a thing
to poor Spoonface who was in bed – which was
me – only I could hear and everything and Dad
said to her for to be philosophical and Mam said
that philosophicals could just go away and that
she did hate God – as basically God is a bastard –
this is what I heard and then I looked up and saw
the wind.

MUSIC: *Maria Callas singing 'Voi lo sapete, O
mamma' from* Cavalleria Rusticana *by Mascagni*

And when we went home the doctor gave me
this book to me – but I can't read so I had to get
Mam to read it to me – and then I found all this
stuff out – like you had to pray to God – and that
this would help get on his good side and even if
you did die then he'd look out for you afterwards
– and in the book it said there was different ways
you can pray – there is like when you get up and
sit and say things – that is one way of praying –
and then there is like you go to the synagogue
and then everybody does it all together and that –
and then there is this different way what was
invented by these people in Poland quite a while
ago – this is when everything you do is a prayer –

and you have to do everything you do the best
you can because it is not just normal, in fact it is
a prayer straight to God – when you smile that is
a prayer – when you talk that's a prayer – and
when you walk that's a prayer – and when you
brush your teeth and when you give someone a
kiss – and Mams and Dads when they go to bed
that is a prayer – and when you pray that is a
prayer – and when you spit, when you suck,
when you laugh, when you dance, when you
snore – everything you do is a prayer – specially
what you do when you meet other people
because all the people in the world are in God's
kingdom – and it doesn't even matter if they're
Jewish – and all the animals, all the birds and bees
and fishes and swans and llamas and piglets and
worms and trees and buses and cars and people
and that – because when the world was made,
God made it out of magic sparks – everything
that there is, was all made of magic sparks – and
all the magic sparks went into things – deep
down and everything has a spark – but it was
quite a while ago since it was made and now the
sparks are deep down inside and the whole point
of being alive – the whole point of living is to
find the spark – and when you meet someone
and say hello – or if you tell them a joke or when

you say that you love them or try and help someone or you see someone who is sad or injured or
maybe they have lost all their money or have
been battered up or maybe they're just a bit glum
or hungry or you ask the time or maybe they've
missed the train – all these people, all they need is
help to find the spark – and the people what
invented this – the Hassid's a long time ago, when
they saw people that were having a chat they saw
the sparks jump in the space in between them –
the sparks were jumping like electricity – sparks
God put there – and the sparks were put there
for each other 'cos God wanted people to find
them in each other – and doing this making
sparks – this was to pray – and the old people a
long time ago they saw the sparks and when
people met and the sparks jumped right up into
the air from the place they were hiding and they
leapt up through the firmament and through the
clouds and past the sun and they shone over the
whole universe – and when people kissed there
were sparks and when people held each other
there were sparks and when they waved as they
were going away in a car there would be sparks
and they would all be prayers – they would all be
prayers for the babies and the sad people with
cancer – and for the kings to be good – and the

experts to be clever – and all the Mams and Dads
and the cleaning ladies and the milkmen – and if
only you could see the spark then there was a
meaning – because what was the meaning of anything? – if you were going to die, what was the
meaning? – all the trees and the bushes and the
famines and wars and disasters and even pencils
or pens – what was the meaning of all these
things? – and the meaning was if you found the
spark – then it would be like electricity – and
you would glow like a light and you would shine
like the sparks and that was the meaning – it was-
n't like an answer or a number or any such – it
was glowing – it was finding the sparks inside
you and setting them free.

This is what it said in this book what the doctor
gave me – the doctor what's Mam was the little
girl whose Mam got shot – and it meant that the
meaning that everybody thought was somewhere
else was right here – and all you had to do was do
the sparks and become like a lightbulb – and the
meaning wasn't that I was going to die but that I
was still alive – and I could make everybody shine
– the bus boys and the milkmen and Mrs Spud –
and I thought, if I wasn't scared of when I wasn't
born why would I be scared of when I wasn't

existed at the other end – you can't feel the end
or touch the end – 'cos it was just nothing – the
end of things is not the problem 'cos there was
really no ends to find – that was the meaning
there are no real ends – only middles, and even if
I was at the end I was still in the middle – 'cos it
wouldn't know it was the end then – because it
would be ended – so everything is in the middle
– even if it was at the middle of an end – it didn't
matter because I'm in it.

And when I looked to my middle and I saw
underneath there was a belly and bones and mus-
cles and veins and cancer and intestines but in the
middle of the middle was sparks – the sparks
what would save me – the sparks what I could
make shine – the sparks that knew there was no
more endings – the sparks what would be as a
huge light in the world and the sparks would fly
up and take me to heaven.

MUSIC: *Maria Callas singing 'Vissi d'arte, vissi
d'amore' from* Tosca *by Puccini*

During the day Mrs Spud comes in and sees
me – she makes me stuff and that and helps out
Mam with the laundry and the cleaning and she

makes the house spick and span and that – if I
was to grow up, I would be like Mrs Spud and
everyday I would clean the fridge and the oven
and the shelves and the steps out to the garden
and some of the skirting boards, but I would
leave the shelves where nobody looks and everything would be clean.

I asked Mrs Spud where I got my cancer from
and she did not know – I said, I think I might
have caught it off God and she said God does not
have cancer as far as we know – I said, maybe he's
just not telling anybody – Mrs Spud says that if
God has got cancer we're all in trouble – I think
maybe he has or he has not.

She said she has a son who is a little angel and
a husband who is dead – he had the cancer too –
only his was of a difference – she did weep when
she told me about him and how when they were
just children they met and he kissed her on the
neck and that – and on those days that the sun
shone forever – she said that the trouble is when
people are around – you forget that they are
quite special and when they are gone it is too late
to tell them and you must always tell them – she
said there was nobody like her husband and that

he was a very kind man to her – and when she
spoke of him you could tell as her eyes were
sparkly and her breath was warm – and although
he was gone away he was also here – and that
every day they had a little chat – and how was
the weather and in heaven it never rained – she
said we would all be there in the same place one
day and maybe I'll get to meet him – I said I
didn't know if I could go to there on account of
being Jewish – but she was sure I would – his
name was Mr Spud.

Then I said that I quite liked the rain when it
was wet and it blew so grey on the ground and I
would watch from the bed when the trees would
weep and bend in the day – and I saw how the
shed wobbled in the wind – and I would see the
cloud for all the silver there was in it – and every
day of the rain, the sun even in its little bits
made the world spark like diamonds and glisten
in the weather – and if I was in heaven there
would be no dull to shine out in the sad days –
but Mrs Spud said she liked the sun and when
she could afford she would go on a nice holiday
in Ibiza – although Jimmy – which is her son –
would not go on account of the price – which is
a shame.

I asked her if she was lonely without poor Mr
Spud – she said a bit and that she would lie and
remember him whenever – but then again we are
not gone – then I said, did she see that there was
blackness and she did not – she said there was
sadness and stuff but that's what there is – but if
you look there is also happiness – like little children having a smile – or someone with a birthday
– and even in a graveyard there might be a little
butterfly flying round the gravestones – and these
are the things what is important – and poor Mr
Spud would be sad in heaven if he thought that
Mrs Spud didn't look at the day and see that in
the trees and in the sky there was a little piece of
heaven.

I felt sad for Mrs Spud as she had three hungry
mouths to feed – her and Jimmy and someone
else – and one day she came into my room to do
the hoovering and I had poo'd in my pants and it
was a disgusting smell and she cleaned my bum
and the bed for me – and I made her a card the
next day – and it said 'I love You Mrs Spud' – and
she cried – and she cried when she got it – she
said, what a lovely card – and I said I did my best
considering the crayons I had which was not very
many and there was no blue so there was no

proper sky – but she said it was quite a beautiful card for a cleaner.

MUSIC: *'Maria Callas singing 'Vissi d'arte, vissi d'amore' from* Tosca

When you think about dying it is very hard to do – it is to think about what is not – to think about everything there is nothing – to not be and never to be again – it is even more than emptiness – if you think of emptiness it is full of nothing and death is more than this – death is even less than nothing – when you think about that you will not be here for your breakfast – and that you will never see Mam or Dad or Mrs Spud – or the telly or hear the sweet singing opera ladies or feel anything any more – but you won't feel sad as there will be nothing to feel of – and that is the weird point – not that there is even anything but there is not even nothing – and that is death.

Sometimes it is scary – but to think that I'll not be is impossible because I'm here – and when I'm not here there'll still be cows and grass and vegetables and radios and telephone machines and cardiologists and soup tins and

cookers and hats and shoes and Walkmans and
Tiny Tears and synagogues and beaches and sun-
shine and walks in the rain and films and music
and my coat and my shoes and cars and under-
pants and necklaces and my Mam and Dad and
flowers – everywhere there'll be something in
the whole world everything will be full except
me – and there isn't even a hole somewhere
where I used to be – and apart from people what
remember me and what I was like there is
nothing missing from when I was here – there is
no space in the universe where people have
dropped out – it is all filled in as full as ever –
there is nothing to know, as is everything that
there is, is all around us – there is nothing to
know because there it is – in the world everything is divided – everything divided one from
the other one, from the many – from the mother
and from the father – there is day and night and
black and white and all these things but in the
very beginning and in the end – everything will
not be divided and there will be no me or you –
there will be no this or that, no little puppy dogs
or anything, there will only be that everything is
the same – and every moment is forever – and it
will shine and it will be everything and nothing
– and that is all there is to know – that all of us

will end up being one – and that is nothing –
and it is endless.

MUSIC: *Maria Callas singing 'Ebben? ne andrò
lontana' from* La Wally *by Catalani*

Blessed and lauded, glorified and lifted and
    exalted and enhanced and elevated and praised
    be the Name of the Holy One,
Blessed be he although he is high above all bless-
    ings, hymns and uplifts that can be voices in
    this world.
May his name be blessed for ever and ever.

(The Kaddish)

THE END